THE
Tattooed Cat

Where Cats and Tattoos Meet

Photography by DAWN MAMIKUNIAN

Written by STEVEN WOOD

JOSEPH TABLER BOOKS

San Diego

*For Billie, whose loving
ministrations have brought
the cats much physical
and spiritual comfort.*

International Standard Book Number: 0-9610330-6-1

Library of Congress Catalog Card Number: 92-60600

Joseph Tabler Books, San Diego, California 92110

Photographs © 1993, Dawn Mamikunian.

© 1993, Joseph Tabler Books. All rights reserved.

Printed in the United States of America.

The Magic Cat

It was an article of faith that the worshipper might become the sacred animal that was the god's representative by being robed in its skin-or by wearing a mask of its head and making sounds and gestures characteristic of its peculiarities, or even by the mere pronunciation of mystical formulæ.

—M. Oldfield Howey

The Cat in Magic, Mythology and Religion

The first recorded appearance of domesticated cats was in Egypt around 2600 BC. Their origin is not certain, but speculation has it that the Egyptians tamed indigenous wild cats for both appearance and performance. Their likenesses were painted on walls and sarcophagi, showing they were used for hunting ducks, for fishing and for killing rats. Cats became revered over time and were assigned the task of watching over the temples. Eventually, they were deified in the image of Bastet, the cat-headed goddess of maternity and femininity.

It was a death sentence to harm a cat in ancient Egypt, even by accident. Egyptians were so attached to their cats that members of a household would shave their eyebrows in mourning when the resident cat died. Cat burials became very extravagant and ritualistic, according to the wealth of the animal's master. One cemetery discovered in the nineteenth century contained the mummified remains of three hundred thousand cats.

The Greeks were the first to import domestic cats to control rodent populations around granaries. Until then, they had relied on the services of weasels, ermines and martens, rapacious predators whose unfortunate appetites were not limited to the rat. They had trouble persuading the Egyptians to part with their cats and eventually resorted to theft, a tactic that resulted in diplomatic difficulties.

The history of the domestic cat in Europe was directly related to the demographics of the rat. The agrarian population soon discovered the benefits of having cats, and their use as rodent killers spread widely. This did not please the Christian Church, however, which considered the cat an undesirable symbol of pagan faith. The cat eventually gained ritualistic importance and became the focus of some decidedly un-Christian rites, a situation the Church found intolerable. The Church went on the offensive, labeling the cat a source of evil and condemning those who showed it friendship. This strategy proved effective until the resident black rat was displaced by the larger, more aggressive brown rat. Once again, the domestic cat rose to the challenge, spreading all the way to North America in the wake of its cunning adversary.

The Church, displeased with the resurgence of the cat and the heresies blossoming throughout Europe, reminded the faithful that cats were the vehicle of the Devil. Through their efforts, it became an accepted fact that witches could assume the shape of a cat. Testimony was elicited from those accused of witchcraft confirming that the servants of Satan sometimes rode upon the backs of cats to conduct their unholy rites on mountain tops. Ecclesiastical leaders emphasized the ability of witches to "shape shift," seeking to arouse fear and hatred among the faithful of pagan religious symbols. The cats, themselves, became objects of superstition and fear, and thousands were sacrificed as a result.

Throughout history, cats were thought to possess powers of divination and healing. The ashes of ritually sacrificed cats were used to cast spells and as remedies for a variety of maladies. One legend has it that on every black cat is a single, white hair, and that if one can pluck it out without being scratched, that person will have a unique talisman and a powerful good luck charm. Telepathic and clairvoyant powers were attributed to cats, who were believed to possess the "evil eye." As talismans or fetishes, cats were killed to bring good fortune to a variety of enterprises. One custom suggested that a living cat be walled up in a building's foundation to assure the strength of the structure, while another called for a cat to be buried alive in a corn field to guarantee a good harvest.

Cats, especially black ones, became omens for all types of misfortune. A black cat, appearing on a sick man's bed, was a sign of impending death, while one crossing a grave indicated that the occupant's soul was in the Devil's possession. In some places, to dream of a cat was an ill omen. In the American South, it was thought that a cat would mutilate a corpse and, if permitted to sniff at a dead body, would bring disaster upon the entire family.

Although many superstitions regarding cats still persist, fear and hatred of them is no longer institutionalized. Cats make many people nervous, perhaps as a result of their willful independence, or their uncomfortable habit of looking a person straight in the eye. They reject restriction, ignore discipline and never respond to their names. They are manipulative, opportunistic, moody and, at times, scornful. Their affection is conditional, and their nature unpredictable. We are entranced by their grace yet appalled by their apparent cruelty, admiring of their keen senses yet faintly irritated with their slothfulness.

Cats are anarchists. They eat our food, sleep on our beds and spray on our furniture. They come and go as they please without so much as an apology, suffering expensive wounds and leaving the dismembered carcasses of their prey in our homes. Still, they hold our imagination just as they did four millennia ago beside the Nile. We are not likely to restore their divine status anytime soon, but we do treat them with deference and, in some cases, reverence. Perhaps it's the power of the old gods, of the moon and the spirit world. And then again, perhaps it's nothing more than envy.

Pushing Ink

The genius of tattooing, its defining quality, is that it shows us that our unconscious must find expression in ways that are not only harmless, but integral to a whole world-view. —Spider Webb

Spider Webb's Pushing Ink:
The Fine Art of Tattooing

The needles are buzzing at Ace Tattoo as they do every evening. The place is cluttered and small, its walls covered with "flash" art, bumper stickers, posters, and Harley Davidson memorabilia. Beneath the red neon sign in the window is a glass case with several animal skulls in it. Next to this, a client offers his arm to Gary, the owner of the shop, who works steadily despite numerous distractions, bantering with the heavily illustrated characters in sleeveless shirts who drop by.

The taciturn kid in the center of the room is tattooing a young military man, whose sunburned face reflects none of the discomfort of the needle. He has brought another couple with him. The wife is pregnant and sits on her husband's lap, chewing gum while staring at herself vacantly in the mirror.

Beyond them, toward the back of the room, Steve is starting to apply ink to one of the large cats he has begun on Chas Taylor's back. He is working from a photograph that is lying on his open briefcase, slowly filling in the intricate markings of Leo's face on the comfortable roll hanging over Chas' blue denim cut-offs. Perched on a stool, Chas rests his forehead on his fist, grimacing as the needle pierces the sensitive skin of his flank. Steve works quickly, constantly wiping away the inky froth that forms in order to check his progress. The black lines are clean and precise, dotted with blood that wells up from the tiny puncture wounds. The cat is starting to take shape.

The sketch of a bigger cat rises from kidney to scapula on the other side of Taylor's back, waiting patiently for ink. The animal sits upright with a prophetic expression, his image dominating the other tattoos. This is Floober, the super cat, and is the most ambitious design on Taylor's back.

Chas is fifty-three years old and has been a client of Steve's for the past eleven years. He describes himself as the artist's most finicky customer, as well as one of his biggest promoters.

Peering in the mirror through his drugstore reading glasses, Chas resembles someone's grandfather, although he admits to disliking children. His short hair and trimmed beard are both gray, and his speech is deliberate and thoughtful. His tattooed shoulders are slightly rounded, giving his entire posture a forward thrust.

Steve pauses, stretches his back, and offers the mirror to Chas. They consult with the photograph and discuss the eyes, referring to a previous problem with another tattoo. A young woman peers around the corner and exclaims in a husky voice, "I saw that man in the newspaper!" She has wild, dark hair and silver rings on most of her fingers. Her shorts are very short, and her sleeveless top very tight. Chas chuckles, enjoying the notoriety. The woman banters with Gary and Steve, then disappears. Steve dips his needle in the ink and begins again.

He is tall and lanky, with his hair pulled back into a long pony tail. He has a ready smile, amused eyes and a wry wit that seems to feed off irony. His own arms are covered with tattoos, revealing his penchant for background design. His concentration is admirable; he works steadily from six in the evening to midnight, seated on a battered chair, unerringly drawing indelible lines on human skin. On top of it all, the curious hang over the counter behind him and comment on his work. It is performance art, and he loves it.

Steve says there is no substitute for human skin, not even pigskin. That means there is no such thing as practice. Botched tattoos can be hidden by incorporating them into other designs or by changing their color. Some skin, like Chas', does not take color well, either because it is dry or lacks contrast. Good artists can tell this before pushing ink.

Steve designs and makes all his own needles from the stainless steel pins entomologists use for mounting insects, silver-soldering them together in different configurations for specific tasks. He makes the normal line needle from three of these pins and a shading needle from two rows of pins—with four pins in one row and three in the other—an eighth of an inch wide. For extremely small detail, as in the castle on Chas' right thigh, Steve uses a single pin. These are not disposable needles and must be sterilized in an autoclave for re-use.

The waiting room is beginning to fill up with an assortment of young people studying the panels of flash art on the walls. Many are already tattooed, others hoping to be, while some are simply curious, peering over the counter to look at the cats before checking out the drawings of skulls, wild animals, and fantasy figures. One massive man with tattoos on his powerful shoulders leans in and says with a grin, "More cats? This guy's crazy!"

Crazy or not, Chas Taylor is covered with cats—his cats. Mimi stares at us with large ink eyes from beneath the epidermis of Taylor's arm. Taco, the Siamese, sits on one shoulder blade, while Arthur, a black cat, prowls the other. Oscar, who is orange, appears in color on Chas' lower leg. There are tattoos of Amelia and Jenny, the latter absorbed by something only she can see and, of course, the developing duo of Floober and Leo.

For the past eighteen years, Chas Taylor's body has been a canvas, its purpose to celebrate the lives and spirits of his cats. He speaks of commitment when he talks about tattoos—a sensible approach when one considers their permanence—and how the experience has brought him closer to his cats. "A tattoo is an expression of one's soul," he says, sagely, suggesting that these images were not hastily conceived.

His first tattoos were small silhouettes, generic cats that were ultimately unsatisfying; he wanted more detail, and he wanted more size. (Chas will tell you that tattooing is addictive— that one or two tattoos is never enough.) The more deeply he became involved with cats, the more the tattoos came to symbolize. The images had to be physically accurate, not simply representative, and had to capture the "cat-sonality" of each animal. This was a tall order, since tattoo artists were more likely to be called upon to draw a tiger than a house cat.

His search for the right artist lead him to Steve Smith, who was relatively new in the business. Steve had drawn all his life and became interested in skin art when he got his first tattoo in the Navy. Steve had never done a house cat before, but had the ability to do the detailed work Chas wanted. Working from a photograph, he designed and drew the head of Chas' first cat, Mimi, a tattoo that looks somewhat primitive compared to his current work. (Chas believes cats of all types are the hardest animals to draw because of the face. He says that Steve is the only artist able to capture the proper expression.)

Steve has finished the work on Leo's face and has begun to apply ink to Floober's impressive form. Since no good pictures of Floober exist, he must work from a photograph of a similar cat in a book. Steve draws quickly and surely, while Chas watches in the mirror, making suggestions about the expression on the cat's face. The telephone on the wall is ringing insistently, but Steve ignores it, and Gary picks it up this time. The shop is getting noisier.

The benign images of the cats on Chas' body contrast sharply with the aggressive, exotic or erotic subjects normally associated with tattooing. Chas does have more conventional tattoos, but believes in keeping them isolated by theme. There is a Chinese dragon, copied from a teacup, on his right thigh with a pentagram resting in the curl of its tail. Next to this is a castle fading into the mist, its roof tiles and stairways a marvel of miniature detail. On the other leg stands a large wizard, which was headless for six months while Chas made up his mind about the face. The result was a wizard who looked like Johnny Carson to some and Chas to others. The wizard is holding typical symbols of his craft, a crystal and a wand crowned with a skull. (Chas points out that the skull does not signify death, but change, as in the Tarot.) Standing beside the wizard is another creature of the occult, a gnome, in a peaked hat with a staff in his hand. There are plans for more dragons, flying ones fashioned after the Indonesian crib angels Chas collects.

Steve has done enough on Floober for the evening and removes the needle from his hand piece. There will be other sittings, three or four perhaps, before he gets the expression Chas wants. The purpose of doing the two cats at once is so Steve can work alternate weeks on one tattoo while the other is healing. The two men discuss money briefly, then Chas pulls on his sleeveless shirt and works his way through the clutter to the door.

The small, garishly painted porch at Ace Tattoo is nearly as crowded as the flash gallery inside, and the red glow from the neon is tinting the faces of the customers at the taco shop below. As Chas descends the stairs, he is talking about his parents, but especially about his mother, who hates tattoos. He tells a story of wearing his shorts to a Sunday brunch at a fine hotel in order to show off his dragon, knowing that it would anger his mother. He can't understand her attitude, particularly about a harmless, personal display like tattooing. Chas rejects the stereotypical "sailor tattoo" resulting from a drunken binge. The people who have serious work done, he maintains, are sober people committed to the artistic/display side of the practice.

Many of Chas' tattoos are presents from friends who understand and support the direction in his life. Some are not. Chas tells the story of the rice cooker, a Christmas gift he exchanged for cash so he could have a small tattoo of Jenny done on his right calf. Some time later, while out to dinner with the friends who had given him the rice cooker, he displayed the tattoo and told them how it had come about. To his surprise, they were upset by this, and one of them was so angry, he refused to speak to Chas. Consistent with his nature, Chas found this amusing and made it a point to share the story with other's, sometimes in the presence of the gift-givers.

Tattooing is not something that happens quickly, or cheaply. Detailed images and intricate designs take time and are very expensive, particularly when applied to something as large as a back piece. Chas believes the back is the best place for a personal statement and tells a great deal about a person. He is eager to have his back complete, but realistic about the cost.

Chas understands the common perception of tattoos and is outspoken regarding the philosophy of the art and the significance of the symbols. Like other heavily illustrated folk, he is proud of his tattoos and displays them readily. For him, they are more than skin deep images of his favorite animal. They are the focus of a belief structure that reaches to his soul.

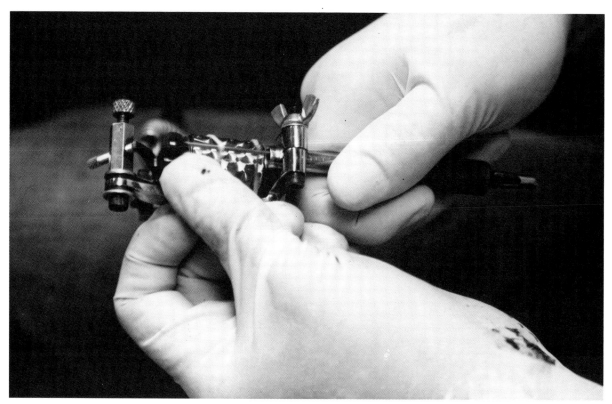

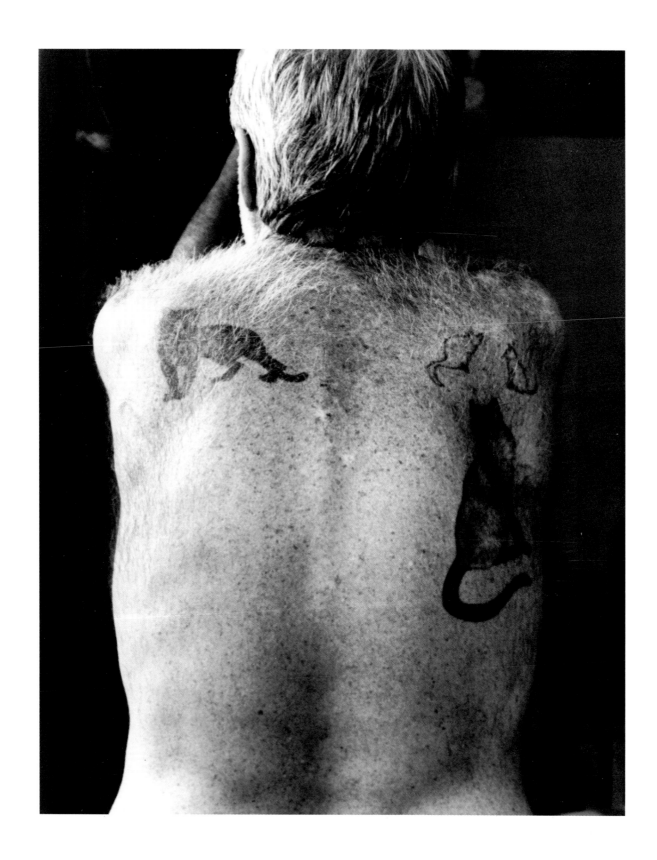

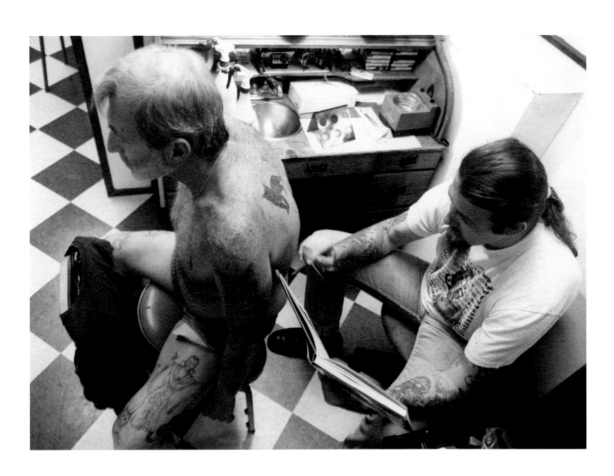

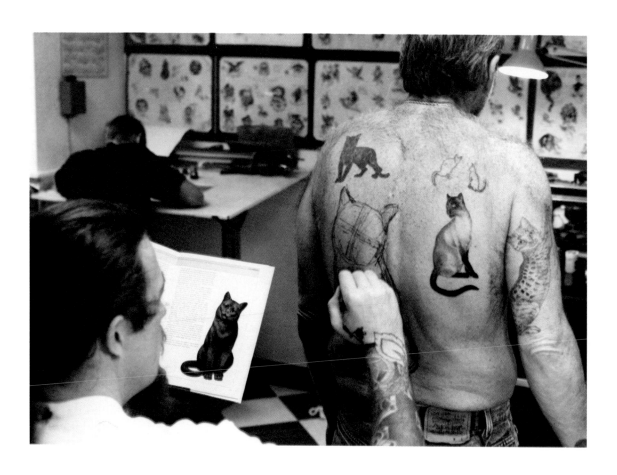

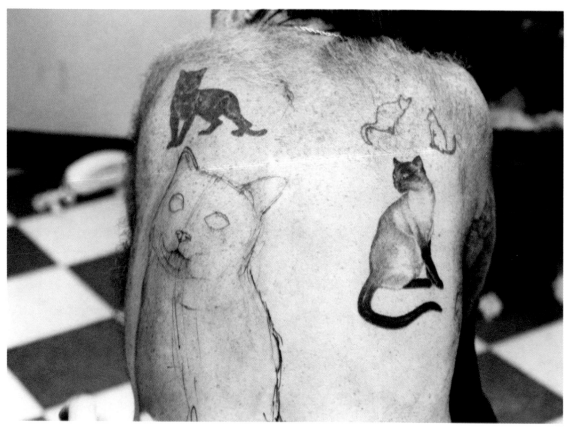

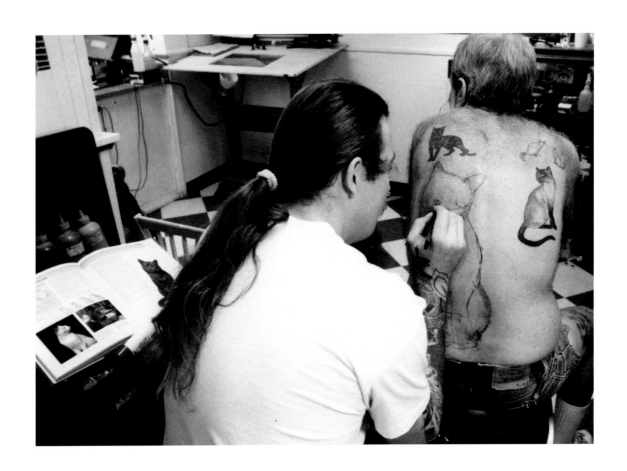

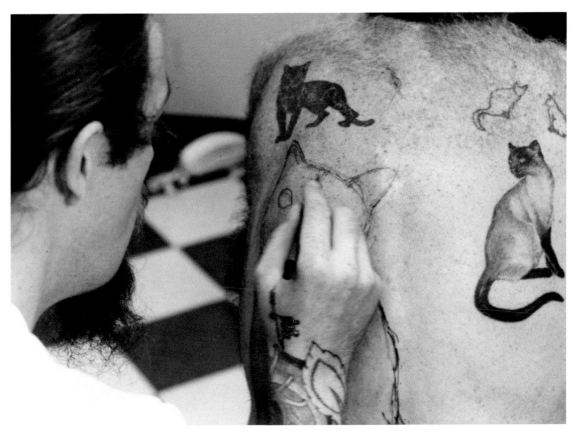

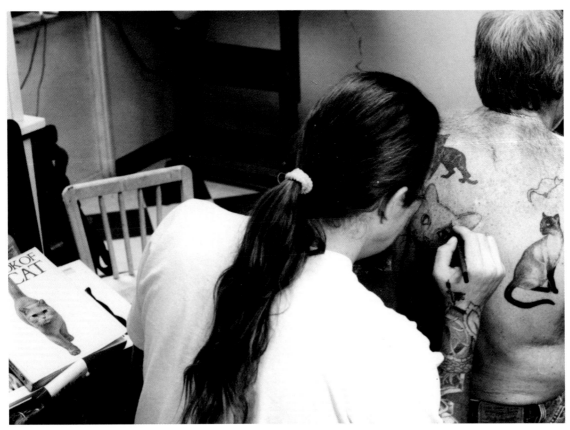

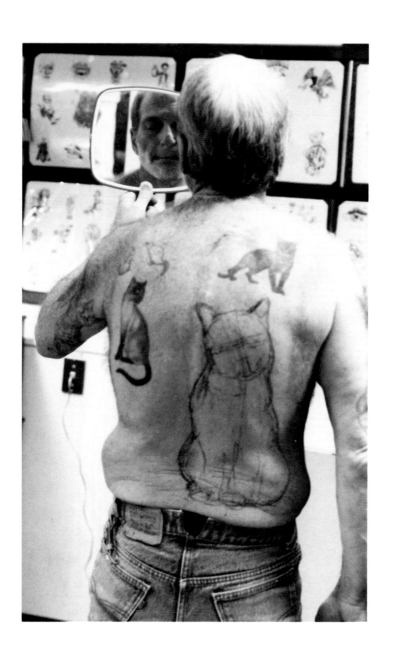 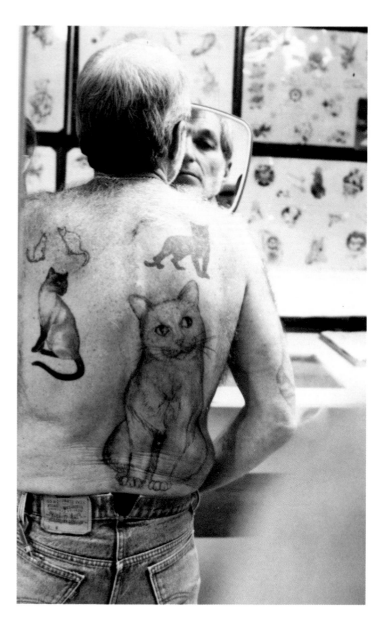

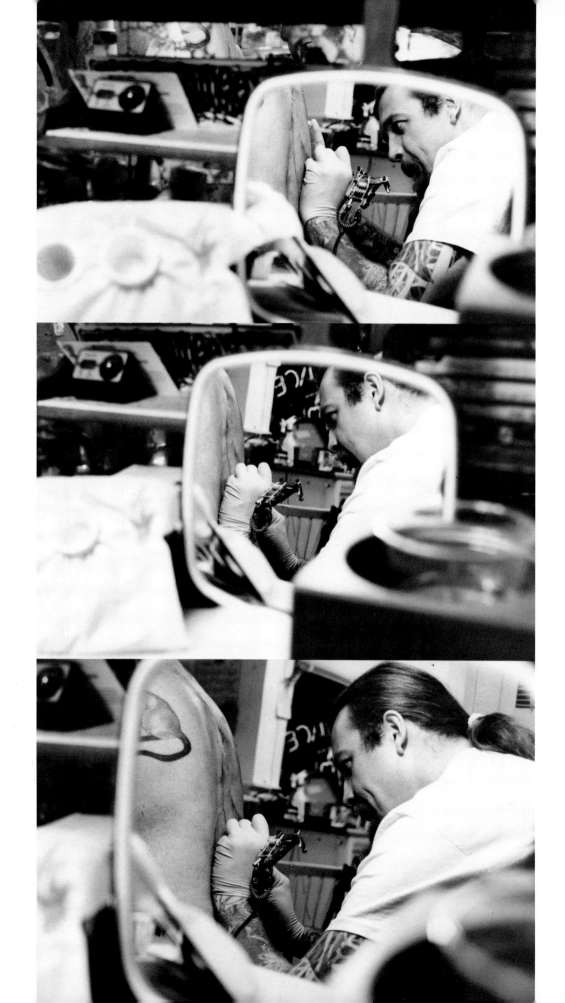

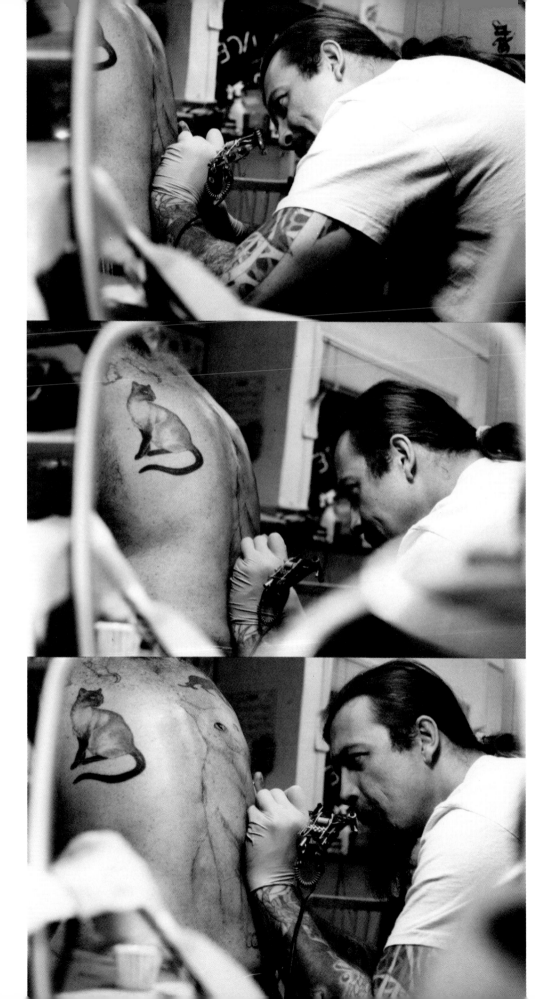

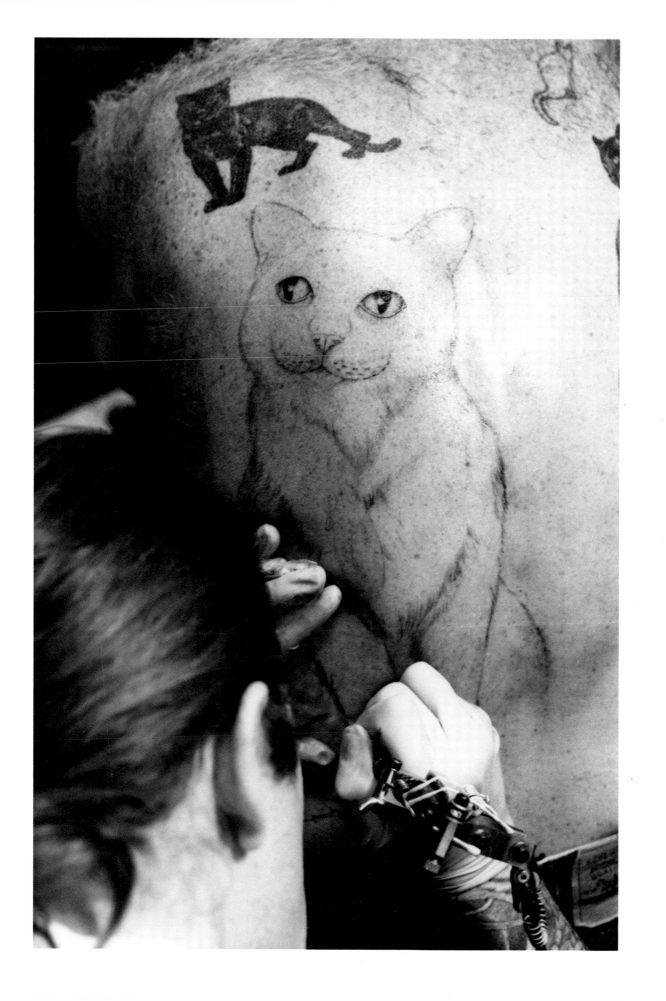

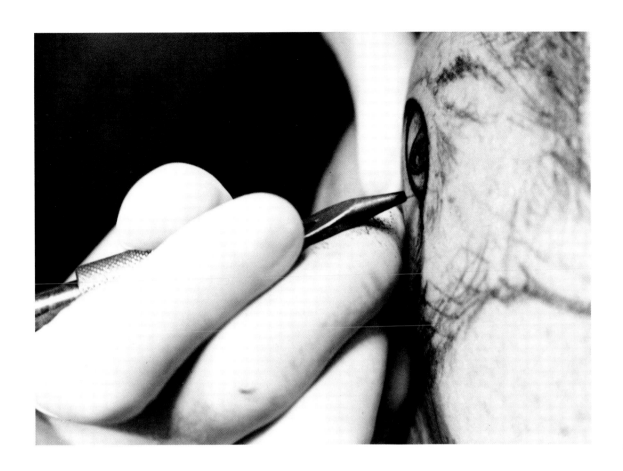

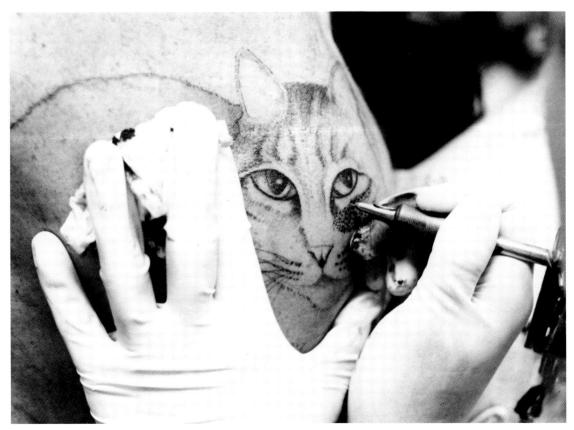

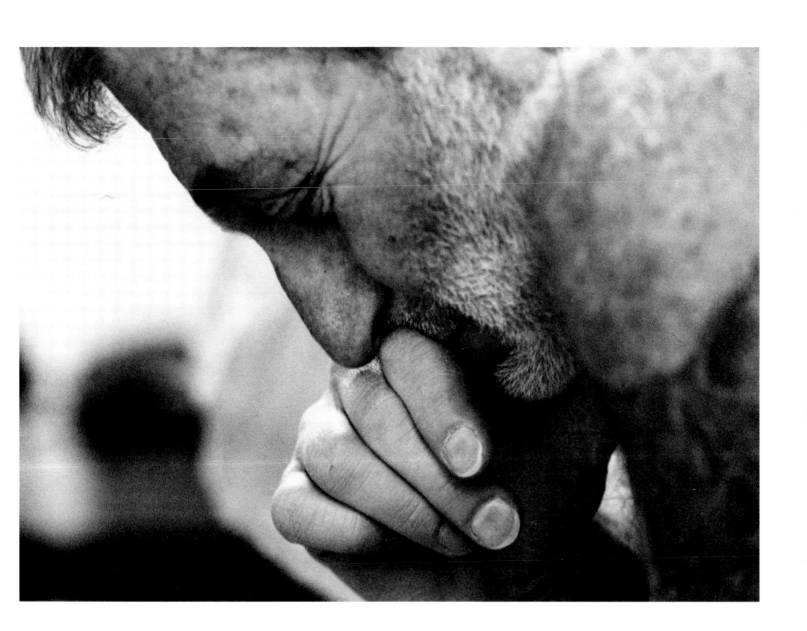

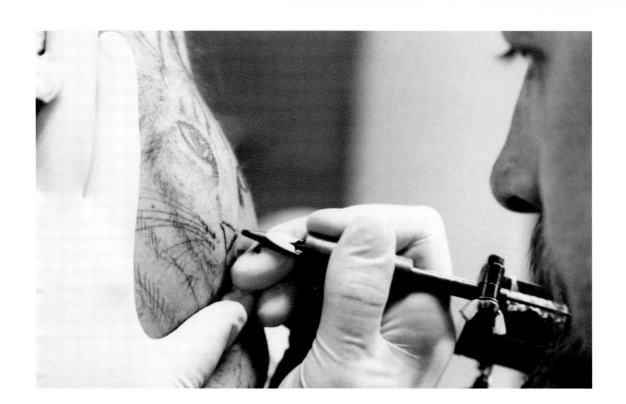

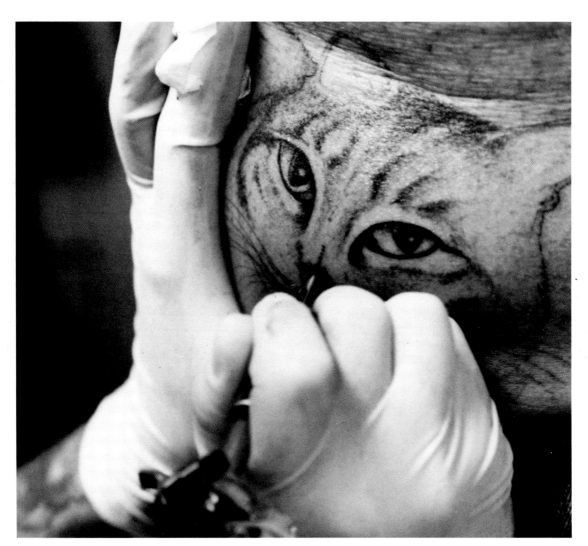

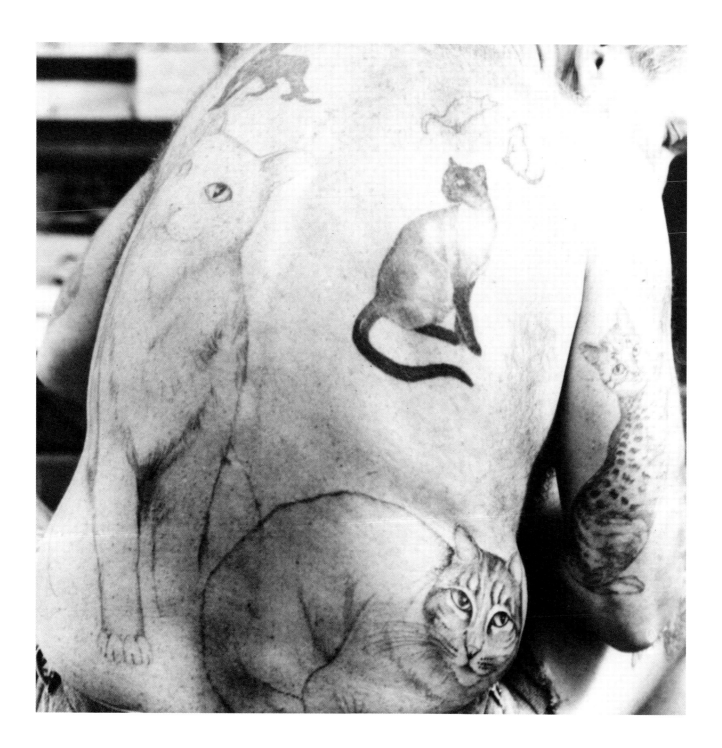

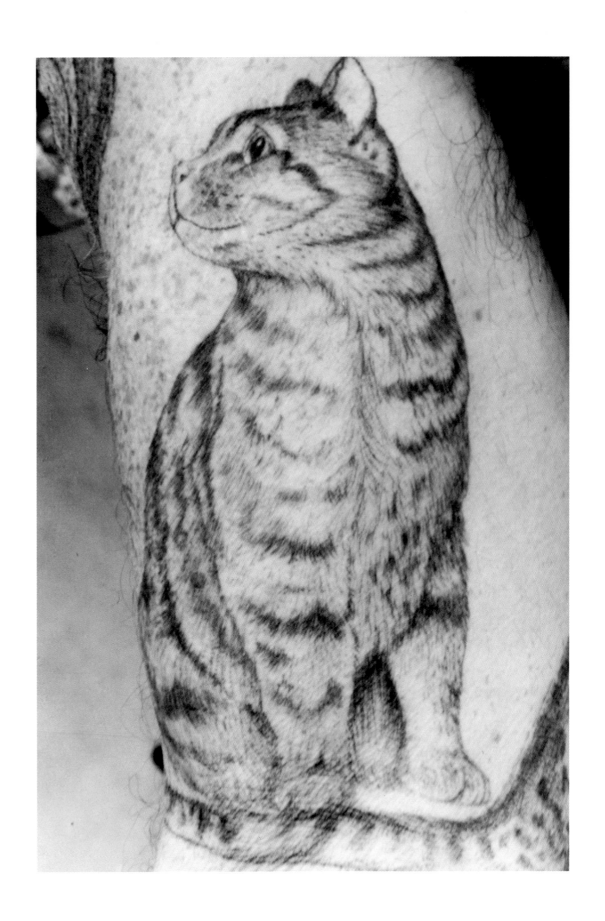

The Fur People

For a Fur Person is a cat whom human beings love in the right way, allowing him to keep his dignity, his reserve and his freedom. And a Fur Person is a cat who has come to love one or, in very exceptional cases, two human beings, and who had decided to stay with them as long as he lives. This can only happen if the human being has imagined part of himself into a cat, just as the cat has imagined part of himself into a human being.

—May Sarton
The Fur Person

Chas Taylor's life is filled with cats. There are cats on his body, cats in his house, and cats sleeping in the old Ford wagon parked at the curb. For twenty-two years, he has rescued, repaired, and nourished more than a dozen cats. Most are recorded in one form or another as unique tattoos accumulated over the past twelve years. He professes to know the minds of his cats and their maladies, as well as their purpose on earth. He treats them as companions, not pets, admiring them as much for their independence as for their perfidy. "You can't control them, and you can't always trust them," Chas says in his deliberate way.

He lives with his long-time girlfriend, Billie, in a neat, one bedroom cottage near the beach that has been modified to accommodate the numerous cats presently living there. A ramp beneath the eaves extends from the porch to a cat door in the bedroom window, and Chas has provided the cats with a "loft" in the kitchen by removing the door to a seldom used, overhead cabinet. The house is filled with cat memorabilia. Posters, statues, lamps, and books are mixed in with the casual furnishings of a Southern California beach rental. On the book case are two brass boxes containing cat ashes, each bearing an inscription and topped with a half-burned cat-head candle. Next to these is a newer urn, a porcelain jar decorated with Chinese dragons that contains the ashes of a lately deceased pet. The books are stacked two deep in most places, but Chas seems to be able to lay his hands on the desired volume without much searching. (He is a well known character in used bookstores.) As saturated as the environment is with cats, there is not a feeling of being overwhelmed by them. The house is vacuumed daily and the furniture appears to have escaped the effects of claw sharpening. During the day, they spread out, involved in their own adventures and are together only at meal time. There are rivalries, to be sure, but nothing disruptive, and all seem to have found their niche, humans included.

It has taken Chas Taylor a long time to get to this point in his life and the journey hasn't always been pleasant. His youth was turbulent and solitary. "I drank a lot and raised a lot of hell," Taylor says. He was a self-described "black sheep," a loner who rejected his family's values. Ghosts fascinated him, and he often wished he were invisible, as if to escape the rejection he felt as a child. By his own admission, Taylor was angry-angry at people, the world, even the universe.

Somewhere along the line, Chas began to mellow. The effects of Billie and the cats upon him were profound, giving his life the dimensions it had lacked. He learned to care, and he learned to grieve, two emotions he had never experienced. Existence seemed to have a scheme, a hierarchy that he sought to understand through his cats. They became a window to another level, a perspective on life and death that made sense to Chas. He used his insight and ability to communicate with the cats to explore this new dimension, finding, as he did so, a system he could embrace.

* * *

Mimi was the first, a tabby kitten Chas found in a snowy parking lot in Illinois. He knew little about cats and, acting on a common bias that identifies all cats as female, named him Mimi. The name stuck. When he was old enough, Chas had him neutered and de-clawed for a life indoors. Together they lived in a one bedroom apartment, and Mimi gave Chas the companionship he needed when things were not going well in his life. Chas moved to a house trailer a year later, where he was living when he met Billie. She moved in and they started looking for another kitten to keep Mimi company.

Chas decided to get a Siamese and they went to look at a litter of four-week old kittens. They selected the liveliest one, a male, which turned out to be a cross between a chocolate and a seal point. (His markings were very light, and he changed color four or five times in the first year.) He was, in Chas' words, "a little spitfire." When they brought him home on Memorial Day of 1974, he chased Mimi around the trailer and climbed the flocked wallpaper. Remembering the problem with naming Mimi, Chas chose the unisex name, "Taco," after "Jim's Taco House," a restaurant Chas and Billie patronized. Taco kept Mimi company, and the two taught each other how to be cats. Taco was vocal, as Siamese tend to be, and required a lot of attention, particularly from humans. Like Mimi, he was neutered and de-clawed to keep him off the wallpaper, something Chas swears he will never do to another cat.

Chas had a job offer from his brother in California and began making preparations to move west. He converted his Ford wagon into a "cat-mobile" for the 2300 mile drive, with a bed and a litter box in the back. Chas fed them less than normal so the long confinement in the car would not be too unpleasant. Billie drove her car, and they loaded the rest of their belongings into a trailer. The cats travelled well, sleeping most of the way, and the trip was nearly without incident. Billie and Chas got separated in St. Louis overnight, and Mimi came scratching at their motel window in Utah, having escaped from the car in an attempt to locate them.

After a week in a San Diego motel, they moved into a one bedroom apartment on the second floor. It had a small porch where the cats were allowed to play, until Mimi discovered he could jump down and go exploring. They hadn't been there long, when they found a gray kitten asleep in a doorway one evening. With the intent of finding him another home, they brought him in for the night and found him to be both playful and affectionate. After running an ad in the newspaper for a couple of days, they decided to keep the cat. They eventually named him Floober, a derivation of Flaubert, since he was a French Chartreuse.

After a year and a half in the apartment, Billie and Chas discussed buying a condo, but were discouraged by the high prices. Chas had always wanted to live aboard a boat, thinking it to be an economical way to live, and convinced Billie they should try it. After several months of looking for something affordable, they bought a thirty-six foot cabin cruiser, stored most of their possessions and moved aboard. The first night was a disaster. Rain leaked through the deck fittings, and Mimi escaped, only to fall into the water while playing with another cat on the dock. The boat would have been tight for a single person, let alone two people and three cats, but they set about to make the arrangements workable. They turned the forepeak berths into a closet and enclosed the bridge in canvas to make a room for the cats. This proved to be a daunting task since the cats could squeeze between the snaps on the canvas. Chas frequently came home to find his cats exploring the marina or hiding aboard other boats.

The cats were confined aboard during the day and allowed supervised play for two hours in the evening. After work, Chas would let them out and watch with dismay as they scattered across the docks. He fished them out of the water on a regular basis, rescued them from various predicaments, and generally suffered as they did. Floober ballooned up to thirty pounds, Taco's fur became greasy, and Mimi took to spraying on things to register his displeasure. Life on board got so bad, Chas and Billie even considered giving the cats away. On top of it all, Chas discovered he disliked boating. "Short of having the Terminator come in and wipe you all out," he says of their first six months aboard the boat, "it was the worst nightmare."

Eventually, Chas and Billie adapted to life aboard and settled into a tolerable routine. The bridge canvas was finally cat-proofed, screens were added for ventilation, and a stack of towels was kept handy for drying off cats that fell into the water. Despite his efforts to make life more pleasant for the cats, the stress on them was considerable, and Chas regrets having subjected them to such confinement. "I know it's part of my karma that I had to do this," he says, "but I would never do it again." The result was a tumor in Mimi between his liver and his pancreas, a condition considered inoperable. Floober's weight gain, thought to be stress related, was actually a symptom of Lymphosarcoma, a terminal disease, which went undetected.

Chas lived on the boat for eight years and moved off after a fight with Billie, who registered her displeasure by piling his possessions on the dock while he was at work. After a night with the cats in the station wagon, he rented the beach cottage and moved in the following day, with a few boxes and no furniture.

The health of his cats quickly became Chas' main concern. Suspecting that something was wrong with Floober, Chas finally took him to the vet and was shocked to learn the cat had not long to live. He was told there was nothing he could do but make the cat comfortable. Floober became listless the day before he died, and Taco gave him a complete bath, something he had never done before. The loss of Floober was devastating to Chas, who had never experienced personal loss before and did not know how to cope with the grief. Billie, seeing how despondent he was, moved into the house with him, a move that turned out to be permanent.

Chas contacted a pet cemetery and made arrangements to have Floober cremated. They suggested that he keep the cat at home for another day so the other cats could understand that Floober had died. Chas put him in a small bed he had made, and Mimi and Taco paid their last respects. Floober's ashes were put in one of the engraved brass boxes that Chas keeps on the book shelf.

Floober's death served to bring Chas and Billie together in more than a physical sense. Their veterinarian, seeing how profoundly they were affected by the death of Floober, introduced them to his theories of reincarnation and suggested they attend a parapsychology class in which his wife was enrolled. They took his advice and were introduced to such experiences as "table-tipping" and channeling. Through a psychic, Chas and Billie connected with Floober's spirit and learned that Floober would not reincarnate for a long time, but would be around to help them with their needs and to protect them. Floober was studying "on the other side," preparing to evolve into a human. This did not surprise Chas, who always believed Floober was special. "He had eyes that could look right through you," Chas reminisces, "like a priest, or someone who was very highly evolved." The cat is never far from Chas' consciousness. For a time, he could feel Floober's presence when riding his motorcycle or when taking a certain route to the vet's office. Even now Chas feels a presence and believes that Floober watches over the other cats.

Mimi's health was deteriorating, and he didn't go far when Chas let the cats out, something he was doing more often. Chas was giving Mimi mega-vitamin therapy and medication, but neither treatment seemed to be having an effect, and the cat continued to lose weight.

Taco, by all reports an emotionally needy cat, seemed to be depressed after Floober's death, as if in mourning. Mimi was failing fast, so Chas and Billie discussed getting another cat. No sooner had Billie expressed a desire for a black cat, than Amelia appeared. (Chas thinks it may have been Floober's influence or that of a spirit-guide.) She was a six month old stray who was immediately welcomed into the family. She had her own emotional problems, however, and kept to herself in the bathroom for the first few weeks. Ironically, Taco and Amelia did not like each other.

Mimi was hanging on to life tenaciously, and Chas was concerned the cat was suffering. The message Chas received from the psychic was to "release" Mimi from his stay in this world. As soon as Chas accepted Mimi's death, the cat immediately began looking for a place to die. As he had done with Floober, Chas put Mimi's body into a box so the other cats could acknowledge his death. The following day, Chas loaded the cats into the car and delivered Mimi to the pet cemetery for cremation. While he was there, he let Taco and Amelia stroll around the grounds so they could pick up the vibrations of the cat spirits there. The entire experience was not nearly as traumatic for Chas as was Floober's passing, since he had prepared himself for Mimi's death. "When it's a cat's time to die, it's going to die," Chas explains, "and that's their karma, just like people." Moreover, Chas had a feeling that Mimi would reincarnate. The ashes were placed in a box identical to Floober's and displayed on the book shelf.

After Chas' birthday in August of 1983, he and Billie went to the Humane Society for another tabby cat. There were two six month old tabbies in the cage, and they knew immediately which one they wanted. When they went to the office, the staff had no record of the cat they had chosen. Chas could not ignore the significance of this, and assumed that a spirit guide had put the cat there for them. They named the cat Leo (after the astrological sign for August) and believe him to be the reincarnation of Mimi.

Chas was in the habit of feeding the neighborhood strays and put a bowl of food out for them every night. A large, white cat they named Shakespeare, who was very skittish and filthy, was a regular customer for these handouts. He had to share the bowl with a black stray Billie named Arthur, who was scarred up from years of combat and who fought with Shakespeare constantly. Chas had noticed that Shakespeare sat under a tree in the backyard when it rained and figured he could use some shelter. Chas built a doghouse from a kit, varnished and carpeted it and set it up under the tree. Not surprisingly, Shakespeare refused to use it, as did the other cats.

Life became more complex as cats were added to the household. Holly, a stray Billie had rescued from euthanasia, was the next cat to take up residence, followed by Arthur, who was bathed, neutered and brought inside. "He was so happy," Chas says of Arthur, "you could even see him beaming and smiling." Holly and Amelia disliked one another immediately, but Arthur and Leo became friends and played together frequently until Leo was injured in a mysterious accident. He came limping home late one night in a state of mild shock with a large chunk of flesh missing from his hip. The injury made him extremely wary, and he never played with the other cats again.

Chas finally had Shakespeare vaccinated and neutered and brought him into the house. He was less impressed by the amenities than Arthur had been and demonstrated his displeasure by using the floor rather than the litter box. As a result, Shakespeare was exempt from the nightly curfew and let out before bedtime. Although he could never adapt to the box, he became a passable lap cat and stayed around a number of years before returning to his previous home in the neighborhood.

The cats' final emancipation came after Chas injured a leg, preventing him from rounding them up each evening. After some discussion, Billie finally convinced him to let the cats come and go as they pleased. Chas installed the ramp and the cat door in the bedroom window and left the station wagon open during the day so the cats could sleep inside. Taco celebrated his new freedom by disappearing for eighteen hours. Chas and Billie were frantic, unaccustomed as they were to having the cats beyond their control. When he returned at three o'clock the next morning, Taco woke them with his howling, before flopping down on the bed with Billie as if nothing had happened.

Billie was working at a substance abuse treatment center and had been feeding some feral cats that came around for a handout. The manager wanted to get rid of the animals, so Billie brought a female home with her. This was Jenny, who, according to Billie, knew she was supposed to be with them the moment she got into the car. Jenny had one kitten with her, which died the following day, apparently from hunger. Chas discovered that Jenny was deaf and had not heard her kitten crying when it was hungry. (He tested her hearing by sneaking up behind her and clapping his hands.) As the most recent arrival in a household with five other cats, she was understandably cranky and tense for several weeks, hissing and growling at everyone until she had established herself. A month later, she disappeared for two weeks, much to Chas and Billie's distress. The next time she disappeared, it was for six weeks, and they assumed she was gone for good. Chas didn't bother to put up signs. "Cats do not get lost," he insists. Jenny, who is an opportunistic wanderer, had simply moved several blocks away to a new home. Chas ran into her one day during his exercise walk, scooped her up, and brought her back to the house. As frustrating as this habit is, Chas realizes there is nothing he can do about it.

There was yet another walk-on, an orange kitten who crossed the street one Sunday and entered the yard as if he belonged there. "There are no accidents," Chas will tell you, suggesting that the kitten was directed there. Chas did not want to become attached to another cat, but Billie persuaded him to let the kitten stay. They bathed away the fleas and named him Oscar. He was a personable, fun-loving animal from the start, playing hard and demanding more than his share of attention. Despite the competition, he got along well with the other cats. As Chas tells it: "An orange cat is a cat's cat."

Magick, the tabby with markings like an ocelot, came from the condo complex across the street. For some reason, he refused to enter his owner's condo, but would go into other houses in the neighborhood. Since he spent a great deal of his time at Chas and Billie's playing with Arthur, they decided to ask if they could adopt him. The owners readily agreed, and Magick (Chas added the "k") moved in permanently. Although he is a very social animal, he knows his home is with Chas and Billie and does not wander.

One day, a mangy refugee that Chas named Long John appeared in the yard for a free meal. "He looked like he came right out of Stephen King's Pet Sematary," remarks Chas, who wanted to catch the cat and clean him up. One eye was swollen shut, his coat was a tangled mess, and one ear was shredded. He looked so bad, a neighbor reported Chas for animal abuse, thinking Long John to be a neglected pet. Chas finally caught the cat one night and kept him in the station wagon until he could be taken to the vet. In addition to the obvious external damage, the vet treated sinus and dental problems, but declined to bathe Long John. Chas brought the cat home after two days with the vet and turned him loose. He disappeared immediately, but returned for hand-outs. Chas has never tried to capture him again.

One of the most intriguing strays in Chas' house is Mr. Cat, a long-haired gray male with yellow eyes who appears and disappears like a ghost. Mr. Cat is feral, yet shows little of the wear and tear of other strays who have sought refuge there. He is a thoughtful, cautious cat who maintains his distance and keeps his eyes open. He followed Holly through the cat door one day and quietly became a part of the routine, apparently with the full cooperation of the other cats. Mr. Cat only allows himself to be petted through the cat door when he is safely perched on the ramp outside. He actually slept on the bed with them one night when he was injured and permitted them to comb out his fur. Chas intends to trap him someday and have him neutered, but until then, he lets Mr. Cat make the rules.

As reluctant as he has been to release control of his cats, he has learned to accept their deaths. When Taco, who had been wasting away from the effects of a tumor at age eighteen, quit eating, Chas had him put down. It was not an easy decision, but one he had prepared himself to make. He had Taco cremated and placed his ashes in the oriental jar sitting on the bookcase beside the two brass urns. Chas reports that the jar, when held, pulsates against the palm with power.

Chas shows equal respect for cats not his own. He makes an attempt to bury any dead cat he comes upon, whenever feasible. Should this be impossible, he will put the animal in a trash can, but dislikes such an ignominious end for a creature he so admires. So far, he has not had a cat killed in the street by his house during the ten years he and Billie have lived there.

For Chas, living with his cats is like living with eight wise men and women. They constantly serve as an example for him: Taco, who elevated himself to another plane before he died; Mr. Cat who acts purely on instinct and intuition to stay alive; and Leo, whose mysterious appearance in their lives suggests a spiritual connection. He is certainly envious of the cats and regrets he cannot live as harmoniously as they do. Over the years, he has learned to deal with them as people, and they have come to be a substitute for a family. Despite his attempts to control the cats over the years, he is finally determined to "live and let live."

Leo & Oscar

Arthur

Leo

Taco

Holly

Jenny

Holly

Oscar

Magick, Holly & Arthur

Holly

Billie

Magick & Jenny

The Other Side

Because man is incomplete within himself, only forming a small fragment of a greater whole, there is always a conscious or unconscious urge within him to seek closer co-ordination and union with that which is greater, but which as yet only assumes a vague and undefined form.

—Aart Jurriaanse
Bridges

Chas Taylor never considered himself to be a spiritual man, yet ever since he was old enough to wonder about existence, he felt there was another dimension beyond the visual, another side to our conscious reality. Until his introduction to the occult (defined by Chas as "hidden") following the death of Floober, Chas had no definable spiritual hierarchy nor any way to discover his own place in the scheme of things. His studies opened up a new and powerful universe that filled his needs and helped explain many of life's mysteries. In the process, he experienced a vast change in his feelings and his outlook, and achieved that which had eluded him for so many years.

It is no surprise that his connection to that universe would be through his cats. Chas feels that cats are on a higher plane than most people, and believes they have an elevated level of awareness, a connection with other dimensions not enjoyed by humans. (There are dumb cats just as there are dumb people and "super animals" that are a cut above the rest.) They have sight that we do not, allowing them to interact with their own "nature guides" inter-dimensionally. According to Chas, cats demonstrate this when they seem absorbed by an invisible presence, playing with apparently empty space as if they see something we do not. Cats do not have solitary souls as humans do, but rather group souls, comprised of the accumulated experiences of many cats. When a cat dies, its soul is added to the aggregate, and when one is born, its soul is a measure of that sum. As the group soul evolves, so do the individuals coming from it, until the aggregate becomes a single, super-animal soul that seldom reincarnates. These super animals are "illuminated beings," so highly evolved that their spirits can come back in human, rather than animal, form. Chas believes Floober to be such an evolved soul.

Karma is very important to Chas. "What goes around, comes around," he is fond of saying. We have free will to make choices, but must live with the repercussions of those choices either in this life or in future incarnations. Chas once relied upon "tools" of divination such as Tarot, Astrology and the I Ching to help plot his course, but finds them unnecessary now, claiming to know intuitively what they reveal. He no longer indulges in "full moon rituals" at the beach, when he would draw things in the sand near the water's edge so the incoming waves could carry his messages into the universe. He believes in a form of predestination, a "lot in life" prescribing our life's path based on our nature. Free will permits us to exercise some options, but no amount of energy or good intentions can right a wrong choice or force a successful change in our natural course.

Formal meditation is no longer an integral part of Chas' life, although he exercises his intuition in much the same fashion on a daily basis. By his own admission, he is not disciplined enough to meditate any more, despite the benefits. Meditation, as he describes it, gives one an awareness of being in another place, not just as a fantasy, but as an interactive experience. When he first learned to meditate, Taco would sit on his lap and distract him. He discovered that he could take Taco with him into an altered state, sharing the vision. He was never able to do this with any of the other cats. Taco reverted to meditation as he approached death, perhaps connecting with spirits like Floober's on the other side, as he prepared to "disconnect" from this life.

Chas often refers to the "guys upstairs," his abbreviation for a spiritual hierarchy that is both nondenominational and multi-ethnic. The chain of command descends from the Supreme Being, to the ascended masters, then through several levels each of initiates, disciples, and aspirants. Somewhere between these groups and humanity in its various stages of "unfoldment," are the guides, little spirit voices that plant ideas in one's mind. They exist on the edge of two dimensions, sharing that place with the "lingering spirits" of animals and people that are sometimes seen fleetingly with our peripheral vision. The bottom of this matrix is occupied by the animal, vegetable, and mineral kingdoms.

Chas' connection to the spiritual realm is achieved through the living cats as well as through his tattoos. When he "centers" on the cats, he can "imagine part of himself into a cat" and connect with their experiences. The tattoos serve a similar function, acting as a focal point of personal energy like a talisman. As he explains it, the power of the symbols engulfs his entire body, and helps him center his mind. "There's a lot of energy that comes from a tattoo," Chas tells us. The cat tattoos are, therefore, doubly powerful, leaving an indelible mark on his entire being.

There is magic in this, not the magic of illusion or incantation, but magic as a "science." Chas defines the two branches of magic, occult science and psychic science, and tells how they derive similar results from disparate methods. Occult science refers to the use of divination (Tarot, Numerology, Astrology, the I Ching, and so forth), while psychic science uses intuition in the study of the unknown. Both involve working in the spirit world with such unseen forces as guides, angels, and fairies.

His cat-imagination has enabled him to develop his intuition, a sophisticated sensitivity that cannot be taught or even fully explained. Chas believes that all people are intuitive, even psychic, but are not aware of their potential and, therefore, never develop it. He applies his sight directly to the cats, demonstrating an awareness of their physical and spiritual condition that is unusually acute. Neighbors often bring their cats to Chas when they suspect a problem, although he does not consider himself to be a "pet psychic." Indeed, he is skeptical of psychics in general and rejects the assertion by some that cats project their experiences pictorially. Chas explains that cats project feelings only, which he picks up in his "gut," and not visual images.

Like any belief structure, cat metaphysics requires a need, tangible benefits, and experiential confirmation. Something was missing from Chas' life—a connection with a force greater than himself, a perception of life that could draw him out of his self pity. Conventional beliefs offered him nothing, based as they were on centuries of restriction, prescription, and penance. He needed something relevant, something that made sense, and something that brought results. What he discovered, was a more forgiving and accessible system, a democratic spirituality stressing unity and a larger role for man in the hierarchy. In the process, his anger diminished, his intuition sharpened, and he began to find a purpose. The proof was all around him, in his cats, in his tattoos, and in daily events. He developed another level of perception and felt the pull of new forces shaping his life.

Despite his journey toward spirituality, Chas Taylor has not found complete peace. The kinship he shares with his cats is not extended to people, most of whom he views with a combination of mistrust and disdain. He is often impatient and willful, but rarely angry. His decision to express himself through tattoos has brought him both notoriety and disapproval, reactions he seems to enjoy. There is something of the rebellious youth left in Chas, and something of the child fascinated by the spirits of the unseen world. It is his karma to have found his way through his cats, and it is their karma to have wandered into his life.

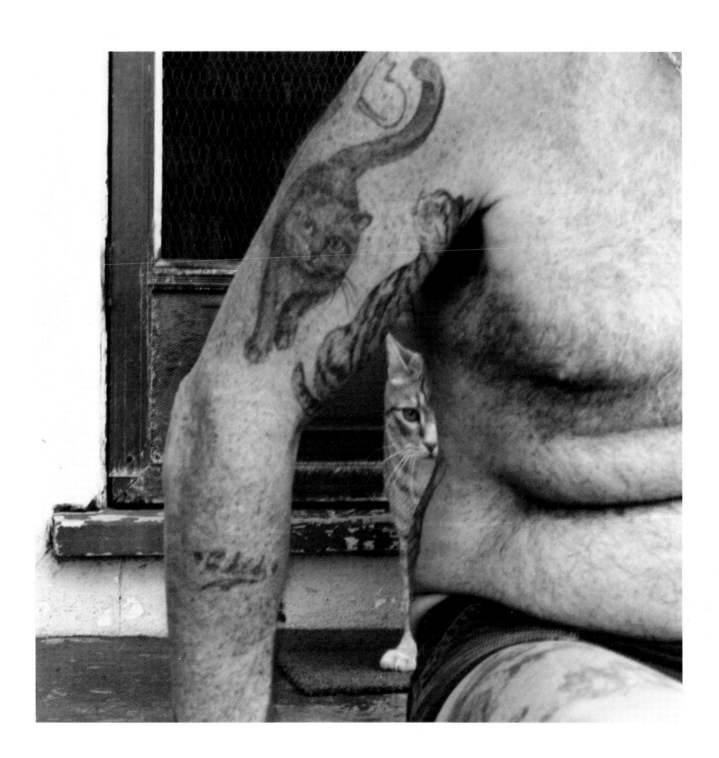

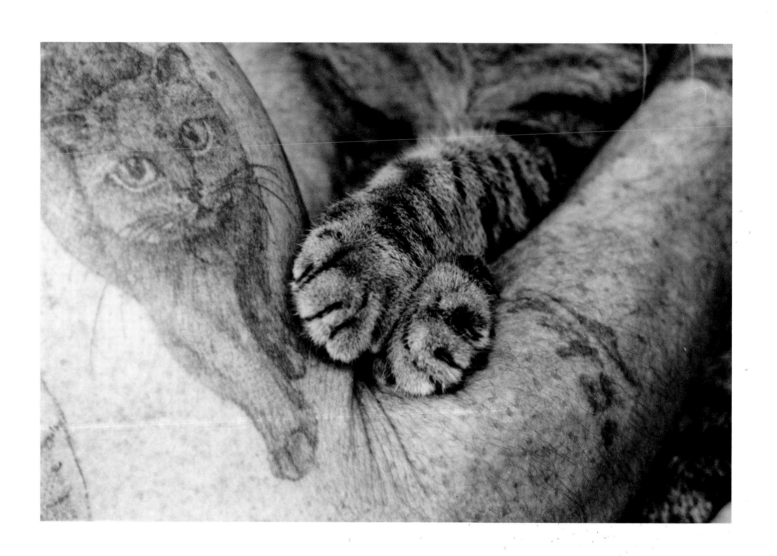

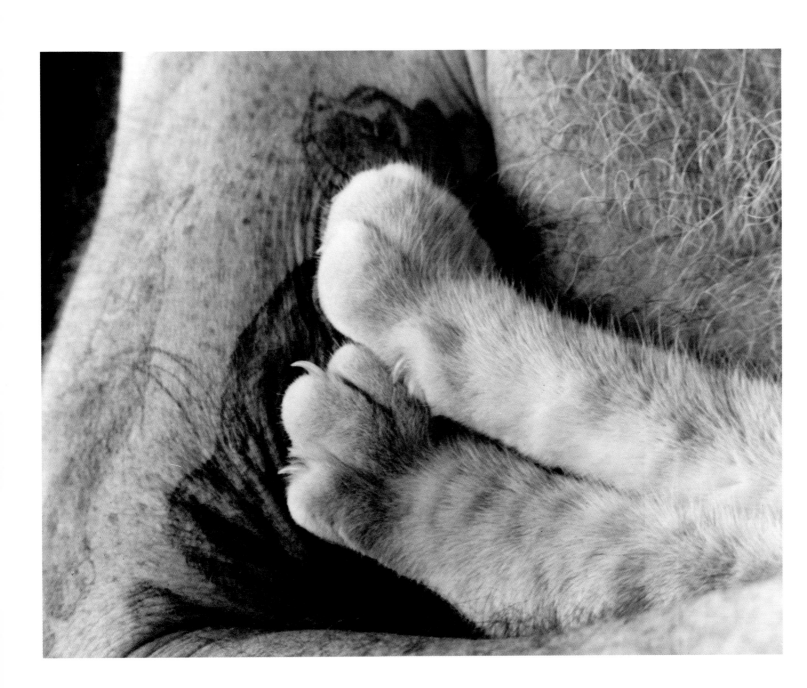

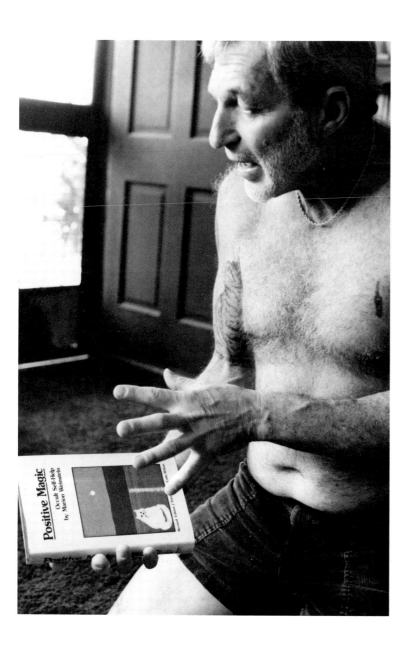 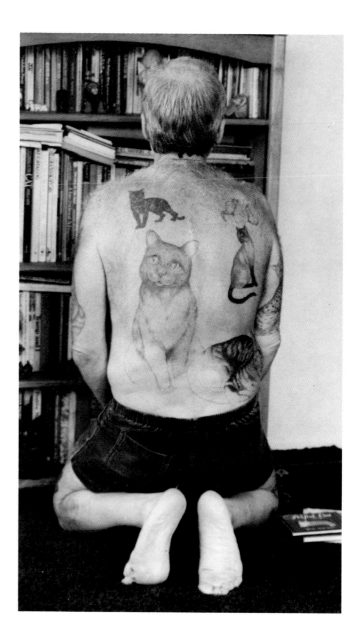

FLOOBER
"A Special Cat"
1975-1982

MIMI
"The King"
1971-1983

Taco

Mimi

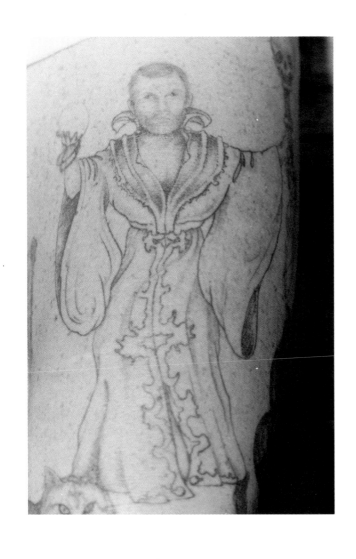

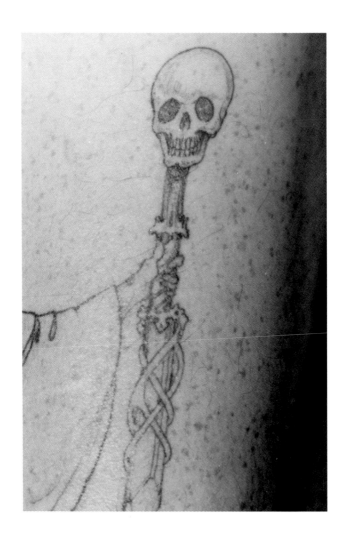

Bibliography

Tattoos

A Selected List of Works in English Compiled by Jan Tonnesen

Barton, F.R. "Tattooing in South Eastern New Guinea." *Journal of the Anthropological Institute of Great Britain and Ireland* (1918).

Best, Elsdon. "The Uhi-Maori, or Native Tattoo Instruments." *Journal of Polynesian Society.* (1904).

Boyle, V. "The Marking of Girls at Ga-Anda." *African Society Journal* (1916).

Buckland, A.W. "On Tattooing." *Journal of the Anthropological Institute of Great Britain and Ireland* (1888).

Burchett, George & Leighton, Peter. *Memoirs of a Tattooist.* London: Oldbourne Book Co., 1958.

Carswell, John. *Coptic Tattoo Designs.* American University in Beruit: Beirut, 1958.

Cowan, James. "Maori Tattooing Survivals: Some Notes on Moco." *Journal of Polynesian Society* (1921).

Davies, G.H. "The Origin of Tattooing." Ibid., 1911.

Dracott, C.H. "Tatuing in India Amongst the Aborigines." *Reliquary and Illustrated Archaeology.* London, 1908.

Ebensten, Hanns. *Pierced Hearts and True Love: The History of Tattooing.* London: Derek Verschoyle, 1953.

Eldridge, C.J. *Early Tattoo Attractions.* Berkeley: Tattoo Archive, 1981.

Eldridge, C.J. *The History of the Tattoo Machine.* Berkeley: Tattoo Archive, 1982.

Fellman, Sandi. *The Japanese Tattoo.* New York: Abbeville Press, 1986.

Fellowes, C.H. *The Tattoo Book.* Princeton: Pyne Press, 1971.

Field, H. *Body Marking in Southwestern Asia.* Cambridge, Mass.: Peabody Museum 1958.

Franks, A.W. "Tattooed Man From Burmah." *Journal of the Anthropological Institute of Great Britain and Ireland* (1873).

Gupte, B.A. "Notes on Female Tattoo Designs in India." *Indian Antiquary.* Bombay, 1902.

Hambly, W.D. *The History of Tattooing and its Significance.* London: H. F. & G. Witherby, 1925.

Handy, Edward Smith Craighill & Handy, Willowdean. *Samoan House Building, Cooking and Tattooing.* Honolulu: Bernice P. Bishop Museum, 1924.

Handy, Willowdean Chatterson. *Tattooing in the Marquesas.* Honolulu: Bernice P. Bishop Museum, 1922.

Hardy, D.E. *Dragon Tattoo Design.* Honolulu: Hardy Marks Publishers, 1988.

Hardy, D.E. *Tattoo Flash.* Honolulu: Hardy Marks Publishers, 1990.

Hardy, D.E. *Tattoo Time #1: New Tribalism #2: Tattoo Magic #3: Music & Sea Tattoos #4: Life & Death Tattoos #5: Art From the Heart.* Honolulu: Hardy Marks Publishers, 1982

Hellgren, Lars. *Tattooing: the Prevalence of Tattooed Persons in Total Populations.* Stockholm: Almquist & Wiksell, 1967.

Hose, Charles & Shelford, R. "Materials for a Study of Tatu in Borneo." *Journal of the Anthropological Institute of Great Britain and Ireland* (1906)

Jaguer, Jeff. *The Tattoo: A Pictorial History.* Horndean, England: Milestone Publishers, Ltd., 1990.

Japan Tattoo Institute. *Japan's Tattoo Arts: Horiyoshi's World 1&2.* Tokyo: Ningen no Kagakusha, 1983.

Kuper, Henry. "Tapitapi, or the Tattooing of Females on Santa Anna and Santa Catalina (Solomon Group)." *Journal of Polynesian Society,* 1926.

Light, Douglas W. *Tattooing: Practices of the Cree Indians.* Calgary, Alberta, Canada: Glenbow-Alberta Institute, 1972.

Lindauer, Gottfried. *Maori Paintings.* Honolulu: East-West Center Press, 1965.

Luard, C.E. "Tattooing in Central India." *Indian Antiquary.* Bombay, 1904.

Morgan, Louis. *The Modern Tattooist.* Berkeley: Published by the author, 1912.

Morse, Albert L. *The Tattooists.* San Francisco: Published by the author, 1977.

Myers, Charles E. "Contributions to Egyptian Anthropology: Tatuing." *Journal of the Anthropological Institute of Great Britain and Ireland* (1903).

O'Reilly, Samuel F. *The Art of Tattooing in Ancient and Modern Times. All About Tattooing and How it is Done in Various Parts of the World.* New York: Published by the author, 1900.

Parry, Albert. *Tattoo: Secrets of a Strange Art, as Practiced by the Natives of the United States.* New York: Simon & Schuster, 1933.

Purdy, D.W. *Tattooing.* London, 1896.

Ray, Miss Cindy. *How to do Good Tattooing.* Ivanhoe, Victoria, Australia: Published by the author, 1963.

Ray, Miss Cindy. *The Story of a Tattooed Girl.* Ivanhoe, Victoria, Australia: Published by the author, 1965.

Richie, Donald & Buruma, Ian. *The Japanese Tattoo.* New York & Tokyo: Weatherhill, 1980.

Richie, Donald. *Japanese Tattooing.* Tokyo: Zufushinsha, 1966.

Richter, Stefan. *Tattoo.* London: Quartet Books, 1985.

Robley, Horatio Gordon. *Moko, or Maori Tattooing.* London: Chapman & Hall, 1896.

Rondinella, G. *The Sign Upon Cain: An Overview of the Controversial Art of Tattooing.* Terni, Italy: Alterocca Editore, 1985.

Rose, Wendy. *Aboriginal Tattooing in California.* Berkeley: Archaeological Research Facility, 1979.

Roth, H. Ling. "Artificial Skin Marking in the Sandwich Islands." *Archiv fur Ethonographie.* Leiden, Holland, 1900.

Roth, H. Ling. "Maori Tatu and Moko," *Journal of the Anthropological Institute of Great Britain and Ireland* (1901).

Roth, H. Ling. "Tatu in the Society Islands," *Journal of the Anthropological Institute of Great Britain and Ireland* (1906).

Rubin, Arnold. *Marks of Civilization; Artistic Transformations of the Human Body.* Los Angeles: Museum of Cultural History, UCLA, 1988.

Sahai, Ganga. "Female Tattooing Amongst the Ghilzais." *Indian Antiquary.* Bombay, 1904.

St. Clair, Leonard L. & Govenar, Alan B. *Stoney Knows How: Life as a Tattoo Artist.* Lexington, Kentucky: University Press of Kentucky, 1981.

Sanders, Clinton R. *Customizing the Body: The Art and Culture of Tattooing.* Philadelphia: Temple University Press, 1989.

Scutt, R.W.B. & Gotch, Christopher. *Art, Sex and Symbol: The Mystery of Tattooing.* New Jersey: A. S. Barnes & Co., 1974.

Simmons, D.R. *Ta Moko: The Art of Maori Tattoo.* Auckland, New Zealand: Reed Methuen, 1986.

Spaulding, Huck. *Tattooing A to Z: A Guide to Successful Tattooing.* Voorheesville, New York: Spaulding and Rogers, Mfg., 1988.

Steur, Patricia. *The Rock Star Tattoo Encyclopedia.* Antwerp: Plastic, 1982.

Sudo, Masato. *Japanese Tattooing-Ransho.* Tokyo, 1985.

Tadasu, I. *The World of Japanese Tattooing.* Tokyo: Haga, 1973.

Taylor, Edith S. & Wallace, William J. *Mohave Tattooing and Face Painting.* Los Angeles: Southwest Museum, 1947.

Teit, James A. *Tattooing and Face & Body Painting of Thompson Indians of British Colombia.* Seattle: Shorey Book Store, 1972.

Tuttle, Lyle. *Tattoo 70.* San Francisco: Tattoo Art Museum, 1970.

van Gulik, W.R. *Irezumi, the Pattern of Dermatography in Japan.* Leiden, Netherlands: Brill, 1982.

Webb, Spider. *Heavily Tattooed Men and Women.* New York: McGraw-Hill, 1976.

Webb, Spider. *Spider Webb's Pushing Ink: The Fine Art of Tattooing.* New York: Simon & Schuster, 1979.

Webb, Spider. *Tattooed Women.* Woodstock/ Voorheesville, New York: R. Mutt Press/Spaulding & Rogers Mfg., 1982.

Wroblewski, Christopher. *Skin Show: The Art and Craft of Tattoo.* New York: Dragon's Dream/Quick Fox, 1981.

Wroblewski, Chris. *Skin Shows: The Art of Tattoo.* London: Virgin Books, 1989.

Wroblewski, Chris. *Skin Shows II.* London & New York: Virgin Books/Carol Publishing Group, 1991.

Wroblewski, Chris. *Tattoo Art.* Wien, Austria: Christian Brandstatter, 1985.

Wroblewski, Chris. *Tattoo: Pigments of the Imagination.* New York: Alfred van der Marck Editions, 1987.

Zeis, Milton. *Secrets of the Art of Tattooing.* Berkeley: Tattoo Archive, 1952.

Zeis, Milton. *Tattooing the World Over.* Rockford, Illinois: Zeis Studio, 1947.

Zucker, Hal. *Tattooed Women and Their Mates.* Philadelphia: Andre Levy, 1955.

Cats

A Selected Bibliography by Chas Taylor

Alexander, Lloyd. *My Five Tigers.* New York: Thomas Crowell, 1956.

Amory, Cleveland. *The Cat And The Curmudgeon.* Boston: Little Brown, 1990.

Amory, Cleveland. *The Cat Who Came For Christmas.* Boston: Little Brown, 1987.

Austinbeir, Joan. *Garbage Can Cat.* Middletown, Conn.: Xerox Education, 1976.

Aymer, Brandt. *The Personality Of The Cat.* New York: Bonanza, 1958.

Baker, Stephen. *How To Live With A Neurotic Cat.* New York: Warner, 1985.

Briggs, Kathanne M. *Nine Lives.* United States: Pantheon, 1980.

Brown, Beth. *All Cats Go To Heaven.* New York: Grosset & Dunlap, 1960.

Bruber, Terry Deroy. *Working Cats.* New York: Lippincott, 1979.

Bryant, Mark. *The Artful Cat.* n.p.: Courage Books, 1991.

Buchwald, Art. *Irving's Delight.* New York: David McKay, 1975.

Burnford, Sheila. *The Incredible Journey.* Boston: Little Brown, 1961.

Camuti, Dr. Louis J. *All My Patients Are Under The Bed.* New York: Simon & Schuster, 1980.

Coatsworth, Elizabeth. *The Cat Who Went To Heaven.* New York: Macmillan, 1958.

Chandoha, Walter. *The Literary Cat.* Philadelphia & New York: Lippincott, 1977.

Clutton-Brock, Juliet. *The British Museums Book Of Cats.* London: British Museum, 1988.

Conrad, Beverly. *Kitty Tales. Bedtime Stories For Cats.* New York: Dell, 1980.

Cosgrove, Stephen. *Catundra.* Los Angeles: Price Stern Sloan, 1978.

Cristol, Vivian. *Good-Time Charlie*. New York : Gramercy, n.d.

Daniels, Mary. *Cat Astrology*. New York: William Morrow, 1976.

Daniels, Mary. *Morris*. New York: Dell, 1974.

Dee, Rhar. *Catnips At Love And Marriage*. New York: Fawcett, 1951.

Fichter, George S. *Cats*. New York: Golden Press, 1973.

Fleischer, Leonore. *The Cat's Pajamas*. New York: Harper & Row, 1982.

Frazier, Anitra. *The Natural Cat*. San Francisco: Harbor Publ., 1981.

Freedley, George. *More Mr. Cat*. New York: Howard Frisch, 1962.

Freedley, George. *Mr. Cat*. New York: Howard Frisch, 1960.

Fritzsche, Helga. *Cats*. Woodbury, New York: Barron's, 1978.

Gallico, Paul. *The Abandoned*. New York: Knopf, 1950.

Gallico, Paul. *Honorable Cat*. New York: Crown 1972.

Gallico, Paul. *The Silent Meow*. New York: Crown, n.d.

Gallico, Paul. *Thomasina*. Garden City, New York: Doubleday, 1957.

Hornaday, Ann. *Cats And Cat Lovers*. Stamford, Conn.: Longmeadow Press, 1988.

Howey, M. Oldfield. *The Cat In Magic, Mythology, And Religion*. London: Bracken Books, 1989.

Howey, Oldfield. *The Cat In The Mysteries Of Religion And Magic*. New York: Castle, 1956.

Ivory, Lesley Anne. *Cats Birthday Book*. Great Britain: Century Benham, 1989.

Joseph, Michael. *Cats Company*. Chicago: Ziff-Davis, 1947.

Joseph, Michael. *Charles*. New York: Prentice Hall, 1952.

Kellino, Pamela & James Mason. *The Cats In Our Lives*. New York: A. A. Wyn, 1949.

Kingrett, Bob. *Live Aboard Cat*. Avalon, Calif.: Kingrett Art Service, 1988.

Kliban, B. *Cat*. New York: Workman Publishing Co., 1975.

Kliban, B. *Cat Calendar Cats*. New York: Workman, 1976.

Knopf, Alfred. *Lords Of The Housetops*. New York: Pocket Books (originally 1921).

Leman, Jill & Martin. *The Perfect Cat*. Bedford Square, London: Pelham Books, 1983.

Lief, Philip. *Cat's Revenge*. New York: Simon & Schuster, 1981.

Lockridge, Richard. *One Lady, Two Cats*. Phila. & New York: Lippincott, 1967.

Loxton, Howard. *The Noble Cat*. New York: Portland House, 1990.

McBride, Chris. *The White Lions Of Timbavati*. New York & London: Paddington Press, 1977.

MacDonald, John D. *The House Guests*. Greenwich, Conn.: Fawcett, 1965.

Mannin, Ethel. *My Cat Sammy*. Bedford Square, London: Michael Joseph, 1971.

Marshall, Bruce. *Thoughts Of My Cats*. Cambridge, Mass.: The Riverside Press, 1954.

Martwick, Bob & Morris. *The Morris Method*. A Book of Cat Care. Star-Kist, 1980.

Mellen, Ida M. *A Practical Cat Book*. New York & London: Charles Scribner's Sons, 1939.

Mellen, Ida M. *The Science And The Mystery Of The Cat*. New York & London: Charles Scriner's Sons, 1940.

Mery, Ferdinand. *Cat Catalog*. New York: Workman, 1976.

Miller, Harry. *Kitten And Cat Care*. New York: Hearthside Press, 1966.

Mooney, Samantha. *The Snowflake In My Hand*. New York: Delacorte, 1983.

Muncaster, Alice L. & Ellen Yanow Sawyer. *The Cat Said Hi*. New York: Crown, 1986.

Patterson, Dr. Francine. *Koko's Kitten*. New York: Scholastic, 1985.

Peak, Michael. *Cat House*. New York: New American Library, 1989.

Pritchard, David. *Kittens*. New York: Knopf, 1922.

Purina. *Cat Care*. St. Louis: Ralston Purina, 1982.

Purina. *With Your New Cat.* St. Louis: Ralston Purina, 1984.

Roth, Beulah. *The Cosmopolitan Cat.* Garden City, New York: Doubleday, 1963.

Sarton, May. *The Fur Person.* New York: New American Library, 1957.

Sayer, Angela. *Encyclopedia Of The Cat.* New York: Crescent Books, 1979.

Schul, Bill. *The Psychic Power Of Animals.* New York: Fawcett, 1977.

Sheehan, Carolyn & Edmund. *Magnifi Cat.* Garden City, New York: Doubleday, 1972.

Smyth, Sir John. *Beloved Cats.* New York: Citadel Press, 1965.

Tovey, Doreen. *Cats In May.* London: Elek Books, 1959.

Tovey, Doreen. *Cats In The Belfry.* New York: Doubleday, 1957.

Towe, Elizabeth. *All Color Book Of Cats.* London: Octopus, 1972.

Tresilian, Liz. *The Cat Horoscope Book.* New York: Dutton, 1967.

Untermyer, Bryna. *Memoir For Mrs. Sullivan.* New York: Simon & Schuster, 1966.

Van Vechten, Carl. *The Tiger In The House.* New York: Alfred Knopf, 1920.

Vesey-Fitzgerald, Brian. *The Cat Owners Encyclopedia.* London: Pelham Books, 1963.

White, Eliza Orne. *Brothers In Fur.* Boston & New York: Houghton Mifflin, 1910.

Wilbourne, Carole C. *Cat Talk.* New York: Macmillan, 1979.

Wilbourne, Carole C. *Cats On The Couch.* New York: Macmillan, 1982.

Wilbourne, Carole C. *Cats Prefer It This Way.* New York: Coward, McCann, Geoghegan, 1976.

Wilbourne, Carole C. *The Inner Cat.* New York: Stein & Day, 1978.

DAWN MAMIKUNIAN studied studio photography at the University of California San Diego and has been involved in photojournalism and multi-ethnic travel photography for twelve years. Her work for an international environmental conference in Moscow was recently featured in a show.

STEVEN WOOD has a Masters degree in English from San Diego State University and has been involved with journalism, technical editing, and copywriting for the past twenty years. Most recently, he edited *Duelling in America* for Joseph Tabler Books.